THE NEW airfryer COOKBOOK

DEVELOPED BY

WILLIAMS SONOMA

TEST KITCHEN

photographs Erin Scott

weldon**owen**

Contents

Curry Spiced Meatballs
with Lemon-Garlic Yogurt Sauce
(page 39)

Welcome to Airfrying

Get ready to rethink everything you know about frying foods. The Philips Airfryer uses patented heat-circulation technology to fry fresh ingredients to crispy, golden brown perfection, all with little or no oil. Food is exposed to constant, circulating heat that cooks quickly and evenly. Airfrying uses only the smallest amount of oil but still produces a nice crisp exterior, so you can eat healthier without giving up the dishes you love.

The Philips Airfryer is ready to go after only a few minutes of preheating time, gives you the option of both preset cooking programs and manual time and temperature settings, alerts you when your food is ready, and then keeps it warm until serving. Large-capacity Airfryers allow you to cook for a crowd, and many models reach beyond frying to achieve expert baking, roasting, and grilling, too.

On the pages that follow, you'll find a primer and plenty of useful tips on how to use the Airfryer to prepare lighter, better-for-you versions of more than 20 popular dishes, from breakfast through dinner and dessert. Try Crab Cake Eggs Benedict (page 25) for a weekend brunch, and a hot Fried Chicken Sandwich with Pickled Onion (page 30) for an unforgettable lunch. Main course selections also cook up lighter than classically fried versions, such as Crispy Fish Tacos (page 36), Curry Spiced Meatballs (page 39), and Salmon Fillet with Tapenade (page 35). Desserts can be air-baked, such as Chocolate Chip Cookie Bars (page 46), or air-fried, such as Banana Bites with Salted Caramel Sauce (page 49). Even many of your favorite snacks, such as Avocado Fries (page 19), BBQ Popcorn Chicken (page 12), and Fried Pickles with Spicy Mayo (page 15), can now be enjoyed nearly guilt-free.

Crab Cakes Eggs Benedict (page 25)

Airfryer Primer

Preparing healthier fried, baked, roasted, and grilled foods in the Airfryer is a simple process. With just a little practice, you'll discover how easy it is to cook with this versatile appliance.

1   Set the Airfryer on a stable, heat-resistant work surface. Plug the unit into a wall outlet.

2   Using the digital touch control panel, press the power button to switch on the appliance, then use the smart presets for your favorite dishes or set the temperature using the up/down arrows. Press the start/pause button on the bottom center of the panel. The set temperature will flash until the temperature is reached; allow at least 3 minutes for preheating.

3   Carefully remove the cooking basket from the preheated Airfryer. Add the food to the basket, then slide the basket back into the Airfryer. Optional Airfryer accessories can also be utilized at this point, such as a nonstick baking pan or a double layer rack (which easily slip inside the basket), or a metal snack cover (which rests atop the basket to reduce spattering and prevent overbrowning).

4   Set the cooking time by pressing the up/down arrows on the control panel. Add a few minutes to the cooking time indicated in the recipe, so you won't have to reset the Airfryer if the food needs to cook longer. If necessary, you can also change the time or temperature at any point during the cooking process. When the timer goes off, the Airfryer will automatically shut off.

5   Unless the recipe directs otherwise, check the food halfway through the cooking time to make certain it is cooking evenly. See Airfryer Tips & Tricks (page 10) for ways to ensure evenly cooked food and to prevent overbrowning and smoking.

6   When the cooking is complete, remove the food from the airfryer with tongs or a long-handled spatula. Work carefully, as the cooking accessories will be very hot and opening the appliance will release hot steam.

Airfryer Tips & Tricks

The recipes in this book were developed using a Philips XXL Airfryer and Philips TurboStar Avance and should work well in any airfyer models, as well as in the Cuisinart Air Fryer Oven and high-performing countertop ovens featuring airfryer modes. Preparing food with an airfryer is easy to do. Employ these simple tips for using and caring for your appliance to maximize your cooking experience.

Shake it

Be sure to open the Airfryer and shake foods around as they "fry" in the machine's basket. This is especially important for smaller foods like fries and chips, which can easily compress. For the best results, rotate the foods every 5–10 minutes.

Don't crowd foods

Give foods plenty of space so the air can circulate effectively. That's what gives you light, crisp results. A "max" line on the cooking basket indicates maximum capacity. Do not stack foods; cook large amounts in batches, or use the double layer rack accessory. Leave at least 1½ inches of headroom when filling the baking dish to prevent food from bubbling over.

Give foods a spray

To ensure foods don't stick to the cooking basket, lightly spray them and/or the basket with cooking spray or add just a bit of oil.

Keep it dry

Pat foods dry before cooking (if they are marinated, for example) to avoid splattering and excess smoke. If necessary, attach the splatter-proof lid (if your airfryer has one) to the cooking basket. Similarly, when cooking high-fat foods like chicken wings, make sure to empty the fat from the bottom of the machine every two or three batches you cook.

Master other cooking methods

The Airfryer isn't just for frying. Some models are also great for other cooking methods, such as baking, roasting, and grilling.

Clean well

After each use, clean the Airfryer thoroughly to remove any oil, as it can cause smoke the next time you use the appliance. When cooking is finished, unplug the airfryer and let it cool. Remove the cooking basket and wash it in a dishwasher or with hot, soapy water and a nonabrasive sponge. Thoroughly clean the interior of the appliance with hot, soapy water and a nonabrasive sponge, then let dry completely before storing. To avoid damaging the electrical components, never submerge the housing in water or rinse it under the tap.

Digital Touch Screen Control Panel
adjusts temperature, time, and
preset cooking programs.

Temperature and Time
can be controlled manually by
pressing the related button, then
making an adjustment using the
Quick Control Dial.

Quick Control Dial
selects preset cooking programs,
temperature, and cooking time.

Keep Warm Button
can be activated at any
time during cooking to
maintain cooked food at
a low, safe heat for up to
30 minutes after the end
of cooking time.

PHILIPS

TurboStar technology

350°

Airfryer Drawer
holds a perforated metal frying basket
over a ridged compartment designed
to capture fat during cooking.

BBQ Popcorn Chicken

Escape the mess of deep-frying popcorn chicken with an easy ten minutes in the Airfryer. For a recipe shortcut, substitute your favorite store-bought barbecue sauce for the homemade version here.

In a mixing bowl, toss the chicken in black pepper and 1 tablespoon salt. Refrigerate for 30 minutes.

In a large bowl, combine the flour, baking powder, and 2 teaspoons salt. In another large bowl, whisk together the buttermilk, Tabasco, and eggs.

Set a wire rack atop a baking sheet. Working in batches, coat the chicken pieces in the flour mixture, shaking off the excess. Dip into the buttermilk mixture, allowing the excess to drip back into the bowl. Transfer again to the flour mixture, turning to coat evenly, and place on the wire rack. Let rest at room temperature for 30 minutes.

Preheat the Airfryer to 400°F.

Coat the chicken pieces with cooking spray. Working in batches, arrange the chicken in a single layer in the cooking basket and insert the basket into the Airfryer. Cook until very crispy and golden brown, about 10 minutes, flipping halfway through.

Meanwhile, make the BBQ sauce: In a small saucepan over medium heat, combine all of the ingredients and simmer until slightly reduced and darkened in color, about 10 minutes.

Transfer the chicken to a bowl, drizzle the BBQ sauce over the top, and toss to coat evenly. Serve right away with any remaining BBQ sauce on the side for dipping.

SERVES 4

2 lb boneless, skinless chicken breasts and thighs, cut into 1-inch pieces

1 tablespoon freshly ground black pepper

Kosher salt

2 cups all-purpose flour

2 tablespoons baking powder

2 cups buttermilk

1 tablespoon Tabasco sauce

2 large eggs

Cooking spray

For the BBQ sauce

⅔ cup ketchup

½ cup apple cider vinegar

¼ cup firmly packed golden brown sugar

2 teaspoons smoked paprika

2 teaspoons granulated garlic

1 teaspoon chili powder

1 teaspoon kosher salt

Pinch of cayenne pepper

Fried Pickles with Spicy Mayo

A light beer-bolstered batter and a quick coating of panko bread crumbs creates a perfect crisp crust for tangy air-fried pickles. Served with spiced mayo for dipping, fried pickles are definite party fare.

Cut the pickles crosswise into thick slices or lengthwise into thick spears. Dry the cut pickles thoroughly on a clean kitchen towel. Set aside.

In a small bowl, combine the flour, baking powder, granulated garlic, and ½ teaspoon of the salt. Add the beer and water and whisk to combine. The batter should be thick but pourable. Set aside.

Spread the cornstarch on a plate. On another plate, combine the panko, the remaining 2 teaspoons salt, and the paprika. Working with a few pickle slices at a time, coat them in the cornstarch, tapping to remove the excess. Dip them in the batter, allowing the excess batter to drip back into the bowl. Transfer to the panko mixture, turning to coat the pickles evenly.

Preheat the Airfryer to 400°F.

Lightly coat the pickles with cooking spray. Working in batches if necessary or using a double layer rack, arrange the pickles in a single layer in the cooking basket and insert the basket into the Airfryer. Cook until crispy and deep golden brown, 8–10 minutes, flipping halfway through and spraying with more oil if the pickles begin to look dry.

Meanwhile, make the spicy mayo: In a small bowl, mix the mayonnaise, sriracha, and a pinch of cayenne.

Serve the pickles with the spicy mayo on the side.

SERVES 6

6 small dill pickles

½ cup all-purpose flour

½ teaspoon baking powder

½ teaspoon granulated garlic

2½ teaspoons kosher salt

¼ cup plus 2 tablespoons dark beer

5 tablespoons water

¼ cup cornstarch

1 cup panko bread crumbs

1 teaspoon paprika

Cooking spray

For the spicy mayo

¾ cup mayonnaise

1 tablespoon sriracha or other hot sauce

Ground cayenne pepper

Goat Cheese & Corn Quesadillas with Tomatillo Salsa

Fresh corn and a mix of goat and Monterey jack cheeses come together in these modern quesadillas. Tomatillo salsa adds an extra punch of flavor.

To make the tomatillo salsa, preheat the oven broiler. Lay the tomatillos cut side down in a single layer on a rimmed baking sheet. Add the garlic cloves and drizzle with the oil. Broil until the tomatillo skins are blistered and juices begin to release, about 7 minutes. Let cool. Remove the skins from the garlic cloves. In a blender, combine the cooled tomatillos and garlic, the onion, cilantro, and jalapeño and blend until smooth. Set aside.

In a large frying pan over medium heat, warm the 2 tablespoons oil. Add the corn and onion and cook, stirring occasionally, until softened, about 8 minutes. Reduce the heat to medium-low, add the minced garlic, and cook, stirring occasionally, until the corn begins to caramelize, about 5 minutes longer. Let cool.

Preheat the Airfryer to 350°F. Spread 2 oz goat cheese on one half of each large flour tortilla. Divide the corn and onion mixture between the tortillas, then sprinkle each one with 2 oz Monterey jack cheese. Fold the tortillas in half to enclose the filling and secure each one with 3 to 4 toothpicks. Coat the quesadillas with cooking spray.

Working in batches if necessary or using a double layer rack, arrange the quesadillas in a single layer in the cooking basket and insert the basket into the Airfryer. Cook until golden and crispy, about 6 minutes.

Serve the quesadillas with tomatillo salsa and sour cream.

SERVES 2

For the tomatillo salsa

1 lb tomatillos, peeled and halved

2 cloves garlic, unpeeled

2 tablespoons olive oil

½ yellow onion, roughly chopped

½ cup cilantro leaves

½ jalapeño pepper, seeded and roughly chopped

2 tablespoons olive oil, plus more as needed

1 cup fresh corn kernels

½ yellow onion, finely diced

1 clove garlic, minced

4 oz goat cheese, softened

2 large or 4 small flour tortillas

4 oz shredded Monterey jack cheese

Cooking spray

Sour cream, for serving

For snack-size servings, substitute four small tortillas for the two large ones and divide the ingredients accordingly.

Patatas Bravas with Aioli & Spicy Tomato Sauce

A spiralizer quickly and easily cuts potatoes into thin, curly slices, then the Airfryer cooks them until nicely crisped on the edges but still tender within. Garlicky aioli and spicy tomato sauce crown this classic Spanish dish.

To make the aioli, whisk the egg yolk and water in a bowl until frothy. Whisking constantly, add the canola oil in a slow, steady stream, followed by the olive oil, until the mixture thickens. Stir in the lemon juice and garlic. Season to taste with salt. Refrigerate until ready to use.

To make the spicy tomato sauce, in a small saucepan over medium heat, warm the olive oil. Add the onion and cook, stirring often, until translucent, about 3 minutes. Add the garlic and cook, stirring, until fragrant, about 1 minute. Add the tomatoes, paprika, and cayenne. Cook, stirring frequently, until thickened, about 10 minutes. Season to taste with salt and black pepper.

Preheat the Airfryer to 400°F.

Using the chipper blade of a spiralizer, spiralize the potatoes, or cut the potatoes lengthwise in half, then cut crosswise into ¼-inch slices. Transfer the potatoes to a bowl, toss with oil, and season with salt and black pepper.

Working in batches, arrange the potatoes in a single layer in the cooking basket. Insert the basket into the Airfryer. Cook until crisp on the outside and tender when pierced with a knife, about 15 minutes, flipping halfway through.

Transfer the potatoes to a platter, top with aioli and spicy tomato sauce, and serve.

SERVES 4

For the aioli

1 large egg yolk

1 teaspoon water

⅓ cup canola oil

¼ cup extra-virgin olive oil

2 teaspoons fresh lemon juice

1 clove garlic, minced

Kosher salt

For the spicy tomato sauce

2 tablespoons extra-virgin olive oil

½ yellow onion, diced

2 cloves garlic, minced

1 can (14.5 oz) crushed tomatoes

1 teaspoon paprika

½ teaspoon cayenne pepper

Kosher salt and freshly ground black pepper

3 Yukon gold potatoes

3 tablespoons extra-virgin olive oil

Za'atar Avocado Fries with Tahini Sauce

Coated with spiced panko bread crumbs and black sesame seeds, air-fried slices of ripe avocado develop a delicately crisp exterior concealing a soft, mellow interior. A lemony tahini sauce strikes the perfect balance of flavors.

To make the tahini sauce, in a small bowl, whisk together the tahini, garlic powder, and lemon zest and juice. Whisk in the water and oil until smooth. Season to taste with salt and pepper.

Preheat the Airfryer to 400°F.

Pit and peel the avocados. Cut into wedges about ½ inch wide. In a bowl, combine the flour, salt, and pepper. In another bowl, lightly beat the eggs. In a third bowl, mix together the panko, za'atar, and sesame seeds. Toss an avocado wedge in the flour mixture to coat, tapping to remove excess. Dip the wedge in the eggs, allowing excess egg to drip off. Toss in the panko mixture to coat. Repeat with the remaining wedges.

Lightly coat the avocado wedges with cooking spray. Working in batches or using a double layer rack, carefully place the wedges in a single layer in the cooking basket and insert the basket into the Airfryer. Cook until golden and crispy, about 10 minutes.

Transfer the fries to a platter and season with salt. Serve right away with tahini sauce and lemon wedges alongside.

SERVES 4

For the tahini sauce

⅓ cup tahini

1 teaspoon garlic powder

Zest and juice of 1 lemon

¼ cup water

¼ cup extra-virgin olive oil

Kosher salt and freshly ground pepper

2 firm but ripe avocados

1 cup all-purpose flour

1 teaspoon kosher salt

½ teaspoon freshly ground pepper

3 large eggs

2 cups panko bread crumbs

2 tablespoons za'atar

2 tablespoons black sesame seeds

Cooking spray

Lemon wedges, for serving

Herby Hasselback Potatoes

Named for the Swedish restaurant where they were first served, Hasselback potatoes become delicately crisp on the outside and meltingly tender on the inside when cooked in the Airfryer. The signature sliced top allows a fragrant herb-and-garlic butter to evenly infuse each potato.

Preheat the Airfryer to 375°F.

Using a sharp knife, cut each potato crosswise into $1/8$-inch slices, stopping just short of cutting all the way through.

In a small bowl, stir together the butter, garlic, parsley, rosemary, and thyme. Season to taste with salt and pepper. Brush the potatoes with half of the butter mixture, making sure to brush between the slices.

Arrange the potatoes in the cooking basket (cutting them crosswise into halves if necessary) and insert the basket into the Airfryer. Cook until the potatoes are golden brown and tender when pierced with a knife, about 30 minutes.

Transfer the potatoes to a platter, brush with the remaining butter mixture, and serve.

SERVES 4

4 Yukon gold potatoes (about 1¼ lb)

½ cup (1 stick) unsalted butter, melted

3 cloves garlic, minced

1 tablespoon minced fresh flat-leaf parsley

1 tablespoon minced rosemary

1 tablespoon minced thyme

Kosher salt and freshly ground pepper

Buffalo Cauliflower with Blue Cheese Dip

Using air instead of oil and cauliflower florets instead of chicken makes this version of the popular snack a lighter alternative to classic buffalo wings. Up the amount of hot sauce in the coating mixture if you like it extra spicy.

Preheat the Airfryer to 325°F.

In a bowl, whisk together the ketchup, hot sauce, egg whites, salt, and pepper. Place the panko in another bowl. Toss the cauliflower florets in the ketchup mixture to coat. Transfer to the panko and coat completely.

Coat the cauliflower with cooking spray. Carefully place in the cooking basket and insert the basket into the Airfryer. Cook until tender, about 20 minutes.

Meanwhile, make the blue cheese dip: In a bowl, mix the sour cream, blue cheese, and garlic until smooth. Season to taste with salt and pepper.

Serve the cauliflower with the blue cheese dip alongside.

SERVES 6

¼ cup ketchup

¼ cup hot sauce, such as Frank's

2 large egg whites

1 teaspoon kosher salt

½ teaspoon freshly ground pepper

3 cups panko bread crumbs

1 head cauliflower, cut into florets

Cooking spray

For the blue cheese dip

1 cup sour cream

½ cup crumbled blue cheese

2 cloves garlic, minced

Kosher salt and freshly ground pepper

Crab Cake Eggs Benedict

A coating of panko bread crumbs results in a crisp crust for these dill-flecked crab cakes topped with a poached egg. Tartar sauce is easy to make at home, but you can substitute it with store-bought if you want to save time.

To make the crab cakes, place the crabmeat in a bowl and season generously with salt and pepper. Add the eggs, mustard, Worcestershire, garlic, and dill and mix until blended. Add the crushed crackers and mix to combine. Divide the batter into 4 equal portions (about ½ cup each) and form into patties. Let chill for 30 minutes.

Meanwhile, make the tartar sauce; set aside.

Warm the oil in a large sauté pan over medium heat. Add the kale and garlic and cook, stirring often, until the kale is wilted, about 2 minutes. Season with salt and pepper. Keep warm.

Preheat the Airfryer to 350°F.

Coat the chilled crab cakes in panko, then coat with cooking spray. Place the patties in a single layer in the cooking basket and insert the basket into the Airfryer. Cook until golden and crisp, about 16 minutes, flipping halfway through. Season with salt.

Meanwhile, poach the eggs as directed.

To serve, divide the sautéed greens between the 4 English muffin halves, then top with the tartar sauce, crab cakes, and poached eggs, dividing them evenly. Season the eggs with salt and pepper. Serve right away with lemon wedges alongside.

SERVES 4

For the crab cakes

½ lb cooked crabmeat

Kosher salt and freshly ground pepper

2 large eggs

1 tablespoon Dijon mustard

1 tablespoon Worcestershire sauce

2 cloves garlic, minced

¼ cup chopped fresh dill

1 cup crushed saltine crackers (about 16 crackers)

1 cup panko bread crumbs

Tartar Sauce (page 51)

2 teaspoons olive oil

4 cups baby kale

2 cloves garlic, thinly sliced

Kosher salt and freshly ground pepper

Cooking spray

4 poached large eggs (page 51)

2 English muffins, halved and toasted

Lemon wedges, for serving

Pancetta & Pea Arancini

Airfrying brings welcome lightness to tender, bite-size balls of pancetta-and pea-studded risotto that are traditionally served deep fried.

In a small sauté pan over medium heat, cook the pancetta until crisp, about 5 minutes per side. Transfer to a plate to cool, then finely chop. Set aside.

In a saucepan over medium heat, warm the 2 tablespoons oil. Add the shallots, garlic, and a pinch each of salt and pepper. Cook until tender, about 3 minutes. Stir in the rice. Cook, stirring, until the rice is translucent, about 3 minutes. Add the wine and stir until absorbed, about 1 minute. Add ½ cup broth and stir until absorbed. Continue to add broth, ½ cup at a time, stirring often until absorbed, until the rice is tender, 20–25 minutes. Remove from the heat and stir in the butter, peas, and pancetta. Season to taste with salt and pepper. Transfer to a baking sheet and spread into a thin layer. Let cool.

Preheat the Airfryer to 400°F.

In a bowl, lightly beat the eggs. In another bowl, stir together the bread crumbs and the remaining ½ cup oil. Form the risotto into 2-tablespoon balls. Dip in the beaten eggs, allowing the excess to drip back into the bowl, then coat in the bread crumb mixture.

Working in batches if necessary or using a double layer rack, carefully place the arancini in a single layer in the cooking basket and insert the basket into the Airfryer. Cook until golden brown and crispy, about 10 minutes.

Transfer the arancini to a platter, season with salt, and sprinkle with Parmesan. Serve right away.

SERVES 6

4 oz pancetta

2 tablespoons extra-virgin olive oil, plus ½ cup

2 shallots, finely diced

1 clove garlic, minced

Kosher salt and freshly ground pepper

1 cup Arborio rice

⅓ cup white wine

4 cups chicken broth

2 tablespoons unsalted butter

¾ cup frozen peas, thawed

2 large eggs

2 cups dried bread crumbs

Shaved Parmesan cheese, for serving

Sesame–Green Onion Wings

For this recipe, select the meaty drum part of the wing (known as a drumette) or the double-boned flat section (known as a wingette), or both.

Preheat the Airfryer to 375°F.

Place the wings in the cooking basket and insert the basket into the Airfryer. Cook until golden and crispy, about 25 minutes, shaking the basket every 5 minutes.

Meanwhile, in a saucepan over medium heat, combine the soy sauce, hoisin sauce, sesame oil, honey, rice vinegar, and garlic. Bring to a gentle simmer and cook, stirring occasionally, until the sauce is reduced by a quarter, about 8 minutes. Reduce the heat if the sauce begins to simmer too vigorously. Remove from the heat and stir in the green onions and sesame seeds.

Transfer the wings to a large serving bowl. Add the sesame–green onion sauce, toss to coat, and serve.

SERVES 6

2 lb chicken wings

¼ cup soy sauce

3 tablespoons hoisin sauce

3 tablespoons toasted sesame oil

2 tablespoons honey

1 tablespoon rice vinegar

1 clove garlic, minced

½ cup thinly sliced green onions

2 tablespoons toasted sesame seeds

Falafel Wraps with Lemon-Garlic Yogurt Sauce

Chickpeas are an excellent source of protein and fiber. Coarsely ground with plenty of seasonings, they create a flavorful base for healthful air-fried falafel.

In a food processor, combine the chickpeas, shallots, garlic, parsley, and cilantro and process until finely chopped. Add the chickpea flour, cumin, coriander, paprika, cayenne, and oil and process until blended; the mixture should have an even consistency but should not be smooth. Season to taste with salt and black pepper.

Preheat the Airfryer to 375°F.

Scoop out even portions of the chickpea mixture about 3 tablespoons in size. Drizzle a small amount of oil onto each portion and roll between your palms into smooth balls and arrange in a single layer in the cooking basket.

Insert the basket into the Airfryer. Cook until golden brown, about 15 minutes, flipping halfway through.

Transfer the falafel to a plate, drizzle with more oil, and season to taste with salt. Place 2 falafel balls in each pita half, then add the tomato slices and lettuce, dividing them evenly. Drizzle each pita half with lemon-garlic yogurt sauce, garnish with mint and dill leaves, and serve right away.

SERVES 6

2 cups dried chickpeas, soaked overnight and drained

2 shallots, halved

2 cloves garlic

¼ cup fresh flat-leaf parsley leaves

¼ cup cilantro leaves

3 tablespoons chickpea flour

2 teaspoons ground cumin

2 teaspoons ground coriander

2 teaspoons smoked paprika

½ teaspoon ground cayenne pepper

2 tablespoons extra-virgin olive oil, plus more for drizzling

Kosher salt and freshly ground black pepper

3 pita breads, warmed and cut in half to form 2 pockets

2 tomatoes, sliced

6 lettuce leaves, shredded

1 cup Lemon-Garlic Yogurt Sauce (page 39)

Fresh mint and dill leaves, for garnish

Tuck the crispy falafel nuggets into halved, pocket-like pita breads, or place atop flatbreads for easy wraps. Add fresh herbs, such as dill and mint, as well as a dash of smoked paprika for extra flavor.

Fried Chicken Sandwiches with Pickled Onion

This air-fried version of classic fried chicken simplifies the process by eliminating deep frying, but still results in a crisp coating and juicy meat. Pickled onion offers a refreshing contrast to the chicken's sweet sauce.

Make the pickled onion as directed. Cover and refrigerate until ready to use.

Preheat the Airfryer to 400°F.

To make the fried chicken, in a bowl, mix the rice flour, salt, baking powder, and pepper. In another bowl, combine the buttermilk, eggs, and cayenne. Working with a few pieces at a time, coat the the chicken thighs in the rice flour mixture, shaking off the excess. Dip in the buttermilk mixture, allowing the excess to drip off. Transfer again to the flour mixture, turning to coat well.

Lightly coat the chicken with cooking spray. Working in batches, carefully place the chicken in a single layer in the cooking basket and insert the basket into the Airfryer. Cook until golden on the outside and cooked through in the center, about 12 minutes, flipping halfway through cooking time.

Transfer the chicken to a platter and season with salt. Brush with sweet chili sauce.

To serve, spread a thin layer of aioli on each side of the brioche buns. Top each bottom bun with pickled onions, a piece of chicken, and ½ cup arugula, then crown with the top side of the bun.

SERVES 4

1 cup Pickled Onion (page 51)

For the fried chicken

2 cups rice flour

1 tablespoon kosher salt

1 tablespoon baking powder

1 teaspoon freshly ground black pepper

1 cup buttermilk

2 large eggs, lightly beaten

½ teaspoon ground cayenne pepper

1 lb boneless, skinless chicken thighs

Cooking spray

½ cup Sweet Chili Sauce (page 33)

½ cup Aioli (page 51)

4 brioche buns, toasted

2 cups arugula

Meaty chicken thighs are the perfect size for airfrying. Lightly coated in a rice flour batter, this version of gluten-free fried chicken is every bit as good as the original.

Fritto Misto with Lemon & Artichokes

Club soda contributes to a light batter for this seafood classic. Dipped first in a thin coating of cornstarch and last in panko crumbs, the pieces of shrimp, calamari, and artichokes develop a crisp and golden air-fried coating.

In a small bowl, combine the flour, baking powder, and 1 teaspoon salt. Add the club soda and whisk to combine. The batter should be a little looser than waffle batter.

Spread the cornstarch on a plate. On another plate, combine the panko, granulated garlic, pepper, and 1 teaspoon salt. Working with a few pieces at a time, coat the squid, shrimp, artichoke hearts, and lemon slices in cornstarch, tapping to remove the excess. Dip in the batter, allowing the excess batter to drip back into the bowl. Transfer to the panko mixture, turning to coat evenly.

Preheat the Airfryer to 400°F.

Lightly coat the fritto misto pieces with cooking spray. Working in batches if necessary or using a double layer rack, arrange in a single layer in the cooking basket and insert the basket into the Airfryer. Cook until crispy and deep golden brown, 8–10 minutes, flipping halfway through and spraying with more oil if the fritto misto begins to look dry.

Transfer to a platter, garnish with the basil and lemon wedges, and serve.

SERVES 4

½ cup all-purpose flour

½ teaspoon baking powder

Kosher salt

1 cup club soda

½ cup cornstarch

1 cup panko bread crumbs

2 teaspoons granulated garlic

1 teaspoon freshly ground pepper

4 oz squid, sliced into ½-inch rings

4 oz medium shrimp, peeled and deveined

4 oz jarred artichoke hearts, drained and halved

1 lemon, halved (1 half very thinly sliced, 1 half wedged for serving)

Cooking spray

3 large basil leaves, thinly sliced, for serving

Coconut Shrimp with Sweet Chili Sauce

Use jumbo shrimp for these crunchy coconut-coated bites. Airfrying results in a crisp golden exterior without the fat of deep frying. A tangy-sweet chili sauce is an excellent accent to the coconut.

To make the sweet chili sauce, in a small bowl, whisk together the garlic, ginger, soy sauce, sesame oil, chili garlic paste, and brown sugar. Set aside.

Preheat the Airfryer to 400°F.

In a bowl, combine the flour with the salt and pepper. In another bowl, lightly beat the eggs. In a third bowl, combine the coconut and panko. Pat the shrimp dry and toss in the flour mixture to evenly coat, shaking off any excess. Dip in the egg mixture to coat, allowing the excess to drip back into the bowl. Transfer to the coconut mixture, turning to coat evenly.

Lightly coat the shrimp with cooking spray. Working in batches if necessary or using a double layer rack, carefully place the shrimp in a single layer in the cooking basket and insert the basket into the Airfryer. Cook until golden and cooked through, 6–8 minutes, flipping halfway through.

Transfer the shrimp to a platter and season with salt. Serve right away with sweet chili sauce.

SERVES 4

For the sweet chili sauce

2 cloves garlic, minced

1-inch piece fresh ginger, peeled and minced

2 tablespoons soy sauce

2 tablespoons toasted sesame oil

2 tablespoons chili garlic paste

2 tablespoons golden brown sugar

1 cup all-purpose flour

1 tablespoon kosher salt

1 teaspoon freshly ground pepper

4 large eggs

⅔ cup shredded unsweetened coconut

⅔ cup panko bread crumbs

1 lb jumbo shrimp, peeled and deveined

Cooking spray

Salmon Fillets with Preserved Lemon Tapenade

Airfrying bestows a light, crisp exterior and tender, juicy interior to quickly cooked salmon fillets. Preserved lemon adds a mild sweetness and depth of flavor to a delicious green olive tapenade for serving alongside.

To make the tapenade, in the bowl of a food processor, combine the olives, anchovies, garlic, preserved lemon and liquid, and capers. Process until well combined. Add the ¼ cup oil and process until smooth. Set aside.

Drizzle 1 teaspoon of the oil over each salmon fillet and season generously with salt and pepper.

Preheat the Airfryer to 400°F.

Coat the airfryer basket liberally with cooking spray. Place the fillets, skin side down, in the cooking basket and insert the basket into the Airfryer. Cook until the desired doneness is reached, about 7 minutes for medium-rare and 10 minutes for medium-well.

Place each salmon fillet on a serving plate and spoon the tapenade on top, dividing it evenly. Sprinkle evenly with parsley and serve with lemon wedges.

SERVES 2

For the tapenade

1 cup pitted green olives

2 anchovy fillets

3 cloves garlic

3 tablespoons roughly chopped preserved lemon plus 3 teaspoons preserving liquid

1 tablespoon capers, drained

¼ cup extra-virgin olive oil

2 teaspoons extra-virgin olive oil

Kosher salt and freshly ground pepper

Cooking spray

2 salmon fillets, about 6 oz each

Chopped fresh flat-leaf parsley and lemon wedges, for serving

Crispy Fish Tacos with Green Onion Crema

A lime-spiked green onion crema is a bright addition to the beer-battered fish in these zesty tacos. Toast the tortillas in a dry pan before filling them.

In a medium bowl, stir together the flour, cornstarch, cumin, chili powder, granulated garlic, salt, and pepper. In another bowl, whisk together the egg and beer.

Set a wire rack atop a baking sheet. Pat the fish dry with paper towels, then cut into 3-by-1-inch strips. Coat the fish in the flour mixture, tapping off the excess. Dip into the egg mixture, allowing excess to drip back into the bowl. Return the fish to the flour mixture and coat thoroughly, tapping off the excess. Place the coated fish on the prepared wire rack.

Preheat the Airfryer to 375°F.

Coat the fish and the airfryer basket liberally with cooking spray. Working in batches, carefully place the fish in a single layer in the basket and insert the basket into the Airfryer. Cook until crispy and golden brown, about 15 minutes, flipping halfway through.

Meanwhile, make the green onion crema: In a small bowl, combine the sour cream with the green onions and lime juice. Season to taste with salt and pepper.

Transfer the fish to a plate and sprinkle with salt and pepper to taste. Spread some crema on each tortilla and top with the fish and green onions. Serve with lime wedges.

SERVES 4–6

¾ cup all-purpose flour

¾ cup cornstarch

2 tablespoons ground cumin

1½ tablespoons chili powder

2 teaspoons granulated garlic

2 teaspoons kosher salt

1 teaspoon freshly ground pepper

1 large egg

5 oz light beer

1 lb firm, skinless white fish fillet, such as cod

Cooking spray

8 corn tortillas, warmed

Lime wedges, for serving

For the green onion crema

1 cup sour cream

½ cup thinly sliced green onions, plus more for serving

Juice of 1 lime

Salt and freshly ground pepper

Add a refreshing zing of flavor to each taco with your own favorite garnishes. Matchsticks of crisp radish and fresh cilantro leaves should be first on the list.

Curry Spiced Meatballs with Lemon-Garlic Yogurt Sauce

Ginger, garlic, and a trio of spices infuse these meatballs with Indian flavors. Airfrying evenly browns the meatballs while keeping them juicy inside. For a lighter version of the dish, swap out the beef and pork for ground turkey or chicken. A lightly dressed herb salad makes a delicious accompaniment.

To make the meatballs, in a medium bowl, mix all of the ingredients, through the cinnamon, until well combined. Scoop out about ¼ cup of the mixture and shape into a ball. Continue with remaining mixture to make a total of 12 meatballs.

Preheat the Airfryer to 400°F.

Lightly coat the meatballs with cooking spray. Working in batches, arrange the meatballs in a single layer in the cooking basket and insert the basket into the Airfryer. Cook until well browned and cooked throughout or an instant-read thermometer inserted into a meatball registers 160°F, about 10 minutes.

Meanwhile, make the lemon-garlic yogurt sauce: In a small bowl, mix together the yogurt, lemon juice, and garlic. Season with salt and pepper to taste.

Transfer the meatballs to a plate and serve with yogurt sauce alongside.

SERVES 3–4

For the meatballs

½ lb ground beef

½ lb ground pork

2 cloves garlic, minced

2 tablespoons Greek yogurt

2 tablespoons panko bread crumbs

1 tablespoon curry powder

2 teaspoons kosher salt

1 teaspoon peeled and minced fresh ginger

1 teaspoon ground cumin

¼ teaspoon ground cinnamon

Cooking spray

For the lemon-garlic yogurt sauce

1 cup Greek yogurt

2 tablespoons fresh lemon juice

2 teaspoons minced garlic

Kosher salt and freshly ground pepper

Fig Jam, Caramelized Onion & Brie Grilled Cheese

The sweetness of fig jam and slow-cooked onion married with creamy melted cheese and peppery arugula makes for an unforgettable sandwich. Brioche is the best choice for a lightly crisped and tender bite, but a good-quality whole wheat or country-style bread will work too.

In a large sauté pan over medium heat, warm the oil. Add the onion and a pinch of salt, reduce the heat to low, and cook, stirring occasionally, until very soft and golden brown, about 20 minutes. Let cool slightly.

Preheat the Airfryer to 350°F.

Spread ½ tablespoon butter on one side of each bread slice and place, buttered side down, on a work surface. Spread ½ tablespoon fig jam on the unbuttered side of each slice. Divide the caramelized onions, Brie, and arugula evenly between 2 of the bread slices, then cover with the remaining 2 bread slices, jam side down.

Place 2 toothpicks at either end of each sandwich. Arrange the sandwiches in the cooking basket and insert the basket into the Airfryer. Cook until the cheese has melted and the bread is crispy and dark golden brown, about 8 minutes.

Transfer the sandwiches to plates, slice in half, and serve.

SERVES 2

¼ cup extra-virgin olive oil

1 yellow onion, thinly sliced

Kosher salt

2 tablespoons unsalted butter, at room temperature

4 slices brioche bread, each about 1 inch thick

2 tablespoons fig jam

¼ lb Brie or sharp cheddar cheese, thinly sliced

¼ cup arugula

Substitute the brie with a good-quality sharp white cheddar for a combination that is equally harmonious but brighter in flavor.

Pork Tonkatsu with Sesame Cabbage Slaw

Pork tonkatsu—panko-encrusted and fried pork cutlets—is one of the most popular Western-style foods in Japan. Cabbage slaw and store-bought tonkatsu sauce are traditional accompaniments.

In a small bowl, stir together the fresh and pickled ginger, grapeseed oil, rice vinegar, sesame oil, and brown sugar. Place the cabbage in a large mixing bowl and pour the ginger mixture over it. Toss to coat. Season to taste with salt and refrigerate until ready to serve.

Preheat the Airfryer to 400°F.

In a bowl, combine the flour with 1 teaspoon salt and the pepper. In another bowl, lightly beat the eggs. In a third bowl, combine the panko with the sesame seeds. Coat the pork in the flour mixture, shaking off any excess. Dip into the eggs, letting any excess drip back into the bowl. Coat evenly in the panko mixture.

Lightly coat the pork with cooking spray. Working in batches, arrange the pork in a single layer in the cooking basket and insert the basket into the Airfryer. Cook until golden and crispy, about 10 minutes, flipping halfway through.

Transfer the pork to a work surface and season with salt. Slice thinly and serve right away with cabbage slaw and lime wedges.

SERVES 4

2-inch piece fresh ginger, peeled and grated

2 tablespoons minced pickled ginger

¼ cup plus 2 tablespoons grapeseed oil or canola oil

3 tablespoons rice vinegar

1 tablespoon toasted sesame oil

2 teaspoons golden brown sugar

4 cups shredded cabbage (purple and green)

Kosher salt

1 cup all-purpose flour

½ teaspoon freshly ground pepper

2 large eggs

2 cups panko bread crumbs

2 tablespoons black sesame seeds

1½ lb boneless pork cutlets, pounded to about ½-inch thickness

Cooking spray

Lime wedges, for serving

Sesame-Ginger Crispy Tofu with Garlic Green Beans

The Airfryer does double duty in this simple dish, frying firm cubes of tofu and then garlicky green beans to tender perfection. The tofu cooks until golden on the outside and the green beans until nicely blistered.

Set a wire rack atop a baking sheet. Place the tofu on the rack and cover with a few layers of paper towel. Place a heavy pot or stack of plates on top of the towels to weight down and drain the water from the tofu. Let rest for 30 minutes.

Meanwhile, make the sesame-ginger sauce: In a bowl, combine the 3 tablespoons oil, the vinegar, soy sauce, ginger, garlic, honey, red pepper flakes, and green onions. Set aside.

To make the green beans, in another bowl, combine the green beans with the 1 tablespoon oil, the garlic, and salt to taste.

Preheat the Airfryer to 375°F.

Cut the tofu into 1-inch cubes. Coat with cooking spray. Place the cubes in the cooking basket and insert the basket into the Airfryer. Cook until the surface is crispy and light brown, 15–20 minutes, flipping halfway through. Transfer to a plate and cover with aluminum foil. Add the green beans to the basket and cook until tender and slightly blistered, about 7 minutes.

Serve the tofu with the green beans, sesame-ginger sauce, and a sprinkling of sesame seeds.

SERVES 6

14 oz extra-firm tofu

Cooking spray

For the sesame-ginger sauce

3 tablespoons sesame oil

2 tablespoons rice vinegar

2 tablespoons soy sauce

1½ teaspoons peeled and minced fresh ginger

1 clove garlic, minced

1 teaspoon honey

¼ teaspoon red pepper flakes

½ cup thinly sliced green onions

For the green beans

½ lb green beans, trimmed

1 tablespoon sesame oil

2 cloves garlic, minced

Kosher salt

Sesame seeds, for garnish

Harissa-Spiced Roast Chicken

When cooked in the Airfryer, whole chicken browns beautifully while the meat remains wonderfully moist. A quick seasoning of harissa, olive oil, and ground cumin applied to the meat before cooking caramelizes as the chicken roasts, adding a mellow hit of spicy flavor.

Preheat the Airfryer to 350°F.

Pat the chicken dry and season generously all over with salt and pepper.

In a small bowl, whisk together the harissa, oil, and cumin. Rub all over the chicken.

Coat the cooking basket with cooking spray. Place the chicken, breast side down, in the cooking basket and insert the basket into the Airfryer. Cook for 30 minutes. Flip the chicken over and continue to cook until an instant-read thermometer inserted into the thickest part of a thigh registers 165°F, 20–25 minutes longer.

Transfer the chicken to a carving board, tent with aluminum foil, and let rest for 10 minutes. Carve and serve right away.

SERVES 4

1 small whole chicken (about 3 lb)

Kosher salt and freshly ground pepper

2 tablespoons harissa paste

2 tablespoons extra-virgin olive oil

1 teaspoon ground cumin

Cooking spray

Chocolate Chip Cookie Bars

This delicious chocolate chip pan cookie is a quick and easy treat you're sure to make again and again. Add ¼ cup chopped toasted walnuts or pecans with the chocolate chips, if desired, or exchange the chocolate for butterscotch chips or chunks of Heath bar.

Preheat the Airfryer to 350°F. Lightly grease the bottom and sides of the Airfryer's nonstick baking dish or an 8" round cake pan.

In a bowl, combine the flour, salt, and baking soda. In the bowl of a stand mixer fitted with the paddle attachment, cream the butter and sugars on medium-high speed until light and fluffy, about 3 minutes. Add the egg, egg yolk, and vanilla and beat until combined, scraping down the sides of the bowl. Add the dry ingredients in two additions, beating until just combined after each addition. Add 1 cup of the chocolate chips and stir to combine.

With dampened hands, press the batter into the prepared pan. Sprinkle evenly with the remaining 2 tablespoons chocolate chips.

Place the baking dish inside the cooking basket and insert the basket into the Airfryer. Bake until golden brown and a toothpick inserted into the center comes out with a few moist crumbs attached, about 20 minutes.

Let cool completely and cut into bars, or, if desired, serve warm with a scoop of vanilla ice cream.

SERVES 6–8

1 cup all-purpose flour

1 teaspoon kosher salt

¼ teaspoon baking soda

½ cup (1 stick) unsalted butter, at room temperature, plus more for greasing

½ cup firmly packed dark brown sugar

⅓ cup granulated sugar

1 large egg plus 1 egg yolk

2 teaspoons vanilla extract

1 cup plus 2 tablespoons semisweet chocolate chips

Vanilla ice cream, for serving (optional)

A last-minute sprinkling of flaky sea salt, such as Maldon, adds refined texture and an extra hit of flavor.

Banana Bites with Salted Caramel Sauce

A thin sugar-encrusted coating and sweet, gushy interior defines these simple air-fried banana bites. Make the salty-sweet caramel sauce and season the chunks of banana in advance, then cook the banana in the Airfryer just before you're ready for dessert.

To make the salted caramel sauce, in a small saucepan over medium heat, combine the sugar and butter. Cook, stirring frequently, until the sugar is dissolved and begins to caramelize, 6–7 minutes; watch carefully to avoid overbrowning. Remove from the heat and add the cream, stirring to incorporate; be careful as the cream may spatter. Stir in the flaky salt. Let cool.

Preheat the Airfryer to 350°F.

Place the coconut oil in a bowl. In another bowl, stir together the sugar, cinnamon, and cardamom. Toss the bananas in the coconut oil to coat, then toss in the cinnamon-sugar until evenly coated.

Working in batches, carefully place the bananas in a single layer in the cooking basket and insert the basket into the Airfryer. Cook the bananas until golden brown, about 6 minutes.

Serve the bananas warm with the salted caramel sauce alongside. Sprinkle with flaky sea salt, if using, and serve.

SERVES 6

For the salted caramel sauce

1 cup sugar

4 tablespoons unsalted butter

½ cup heavy cream

1 teaspoon flaky sea salt or kosher salt

½ cup coconut oil, melted

1 cup sugar

2 tablespoons ground cinnamon

1 teaspoon ground cardamom

3 bananas, peeled and sliced on the bias into 2-inch pieces

Flaky sea salt, for garnish (optional)

Spiced Apple Pockets

Lightly spiced wedges of apple fill these golden pastry squares. Tart, crisp Pink Lady or sweeter Fuji apples are an excellent choice, but any good baking apple will do.

In a medium saucepan over medium heat, combine the water, brown sugar, and butter. Cook, stirring, until the sugar dissolves, about 3 minutes. Add the apples, cinnamon, cardamom, and salt and stir to combine. Cook until the apples are fork-tender and the liquid is thickened, about 8 minutes. Let stand at room temperature until cool.

On a floured work surface, roll out the puff pastry to a 16 x 16" square. Cut the square into 8 rectangles by cutting in half lengthwise and then crosswise into quarters. Brush the edges of each rectangle with some of the beaten egg, then place about 2 tablespoons of the apple filling in the center. Fold the rectangle in half crosswise to enclose the filling. Use a fork to seal and crimp the edges. Cut a small slit in the top of each pocket, then brush the top with more of the beaten egg and sprinkle with turbinado sugar. Place the pockets on a baking sheet and freeze for at least 15 minutes. Use right away or transfer to a heavy-duty, locktop plastic bag and freeze for at least 15 minutes or for up to 3 months.

Preheat the Airfryer to 400°F.

Working in batches, place the pockets in a single layer in the cooking basket and insert the basket into the Airfryer. Cook until the pockets are golden brown and puffed, about 8 minutes (or 13 minutes if frozen).

Serve warm with a scoop of vanilla ice cream on top.

SERVES 8

½ cup water

⅓ cup firmly packed golden brown sugar

3 tablespoons unsalted butter

1 lb Pink Lady or Fuji apples, cored and thinly sliced

1 teaspoon ground cinnamon

½ teaspoon ground cardamom

¼ teaspoon kosher salt

1 package (about 1 lb) puff pastry, thawed

1 large egg, lightly beaten

Turbinado sugar, for sprinkling

Vanilla ice cream, for serving

Basic Recipes

AIOLI

1 egg yolk

1 teaspoon water

⅓ cup canola oil

¼ cup extra-virgin olive oil

2 teaspoons lemon juice

1 clove garlic, minced

Kosher salt

In a bowl, whisk together the egg yolk and water until frothy. Whisking constantly, slowly add the canola oil, followed by the olive oil, in a thin, steady stream, whisking until the mixture thickens. Stir in the lemon juice and garlic and season to taste with salt. Cover and refrigerate until ready to use.

MAKES ABOUT ¾ CUP

PICKLED ONION

1 small red onion, thinly sliced

1 cup white vinegar

½ cup water

½ cup firmly packed golden brown sugar

1 tablespoon kosher salt

Place the sliced onion in a nonreactive bowl. In a saucepan, combine the vinegar, water, brown sugar, and salt. Bring to a simmer and stir to dissolve the sugar and salt. Pour the liquid over the onion. Let cool. Cover and refrigerate until ready to use.

MAKES ABOUT 1 CUP

TARTAR SAUCE

1 cup Aioli (recipe at left) or store-bought mayonnaise

2 tablespoons chopped cornichons

1 tablespoon fresh minced tarragon

1 tablespoon fresh lemon juice

1 teaspoon Dijon mustard

Kosher salt and freshly ground pepper

In a bowl, stir together the aioli, cornichons, tarragon, lemon juice, and mustard. Season to taste with salt and pepper. Thin with 1 teaspoon of water at a time to the desired consistency. Cover and refrigerate until ready to use.

MAKES ABOUT 1¼ CUP

POACHED EGGS

1 teaspoon white vinegar

½ teaspoon kosher salt

4 large eggs

Fill a large nonstick frying pan three-fourths full with water and bring to a simmer over medium heat. Add the vinegar and salt. Crack the eggs into individual cups and gently slide the eggs into the simmering water, spacing them evenly apart. Cook until the whites are set, 2–3 minutes. Using a slotted spoon, transfer the eggs to paper towels to drain, then use as directed.

SERVES 4

Index

Hot air from the Airfryer results in bar cookies that are light and fluffy in texture. Cut into pieces and serve plain or top with a scoop of your favorite ice cream.

The New Airfryer Cookbook

Conceived and produced by Weldon Owen
in collaboration with Williams Sonoma, Inc.
3250 Van Ness Avenue, San Francisco, CA 94109

A WELDON OWEN PRODUCTION
1150 Brickyard Cove Road
Richmond, CA 94801
www.weldonowen.com

Printed in China
First printed in 2018
10 9 8 7

Library of Congress Cataloging-in-Publication
data is available.

ISBN 978-1-68188-465-3

WELDON OWEN INTERNATIONAL
President & Publisher Roger Shaw
SVP, Sales & Marketing Amy Kaneko

Associate Publisher Amy Marr
Senior Editor Lisa Atwood

Creative Director Kelly Booth
Art Director Marisa Kwek
Designer Meghan Hildebrand

Production Director Michelle Duggan
Imaging Manager Don Hill

Photographer Erin Scott
Food Stylist Lillian Kang
Prop Stylist Kerrie Sherrell Walsh

ACKNOWLEDGMENTS

Weldon Owen International wishes to thank the following people for their
generous support in producing this book: Barbara Brenner, Lou Bustamante,
Josephine Hsu, Marisa Kwek, Eve Lynch, Rachel Markowitz, Alexis Mersel,
Nicola Parisi, Elizabeth Parson, Emerson Tenney, and Andrea Trezza..